ROYAL OPERA HOUSE

POCKET PHOTO BOOKS

ROYAL OPERA HOUSE

HARRY CORY WRIGHT

INTRODUCTION BY ALEX BEARD
CHIEF EXECUTIVE, ROYAL OPERA HOUSE

INTRODUCTION
BY ALEX BEARD

The Royal Opera House sits at the heart of one of the most diverse and vibrant cities in the world. As I cross the cobblestones of Covent Garden market, in the quiet before the crowds arrive, I sometimes reflect on the history of this three-acre site. The first theatre here opened in 1732, since when – with a few remarkably brief interruptions when the theatre had to be completely rebuilt after two disastrous fires – we have been a place of landmark experiences: the first public piano performance in England; premières of several of Handel's operas; and the first use of limelight, a Victorian innovation that allowed performers to be placed quite literally in the spotlight. But there is also a daily accomplishment: the transformation created by exceptional artists on our stages, moving us, the audience, to feel differently about ourselves and our place in the world.

The Royal Opera House has a rich history, but what has changed over recent years is equally important. The building is a place not only where people come for an evening performance or an occasional matinée, but also where visitors can now spend the day, enjoying tours and exhibitions, daytime performances and workshops, or just having something to eat and drink. Our aim remains to open up this world-renowned building that has been a major part of London's Theatreland for generations, to connect our extended community of dancers, singers, musicians, craftspeople, supporters and audience members, to offer a taste of the remarkable creativity at play here, and in the process to inspire many more people to connect with our art forms.

'a state-of-the-art theatre in a heritage building'

The building is animated throughout the day and night. Performances usually finish around 10.30 pm, but that's not the end of the working day for the backstage teams, who tend not to leave until close to midnight. Early most mornings I enter through the Stage Door in Floral Street, the same entrance used by Maria Callas, Margot Fonteyn, John Vickers and Carlos Kleiber. Although I don't bump into many performers at this time of day, many of the technical team are on the early shift, looking forward to a freshly cooked breakfast in the staff canteen. Visitors often comment on the building's labyrinth of corridors, the result of creating a state-of-the-art theatre in a heritage building. As I make my way to my desk, I pass a colourful display of historic production posters and possibly a harp in its case or a frothy tower of tutus arranged for storage on a wooden pole. Sometimes, passing a rack of exquisitely tailored costumes, I'll take a peek at some of the tags sewn into them where you would usually find the label in an off-the-peg garment: here are listed the name of the production, the role for which it was created, and the performers who have recently worn it. It is thrilling to see even these ghosts of a performance, these hints of iconic characters that come so fully to life on stage.

I see three or four performances a week, some in the grand velvet-and-gilt main auditorium and others in our recently refurbished Linbury Theatre. It has been a joy to convert the Linbury from a rather basic black box into a contemporary version of a Renaissance playhouse: a completely sustainable, walnut-panelled four-hundred-seat space with excellent acoustics and illuminated only with LED lighting. Our ambition was to create a space of equal quality to the main stage but with a different character, a place where we could perform compelling works on a more intimate scale. Directors, composers and choreographers have the chance to create new works in the Linbury before they are ready to fill an auditorium of more than two thousand people. And it works both ways, with some of our most established creatives gravitating towards the Linbury for the opportunity it offers to connect closely with the audience.

> '*a contemporary version of*
> *a Renaissance playhouse*'

In the morning, light pours into the Linbury Foyer from Bow Street, and if passers-by glance in they will spot a grand piano at the foot of the stairs. Later in the day they could see it being played to accompany a free lunchtime concert or dance performance. At our first-ever Live at Lunch performance, Liubov Ulybysheva, a cellist from the Orchestra of the Royal Opera House, was playing an uncompromising programme of pieces by Delius and John Ireland, accompanied by John Paul Elkins on the piano. I was sitting on the stairs listening, and at a pause in the performance a profoundly deaf member of the audience asked if he could put his hands on the body of the piano. It was a deeply moving moment, and one that wouldn't have been possible in a more formal space.

The Linbury Foyer is a bright open space, blending polished marble and dark wood in a way that connects it architecturally to the Linbury Theatre. As in all our front-of-house spaces, we display elements of our art forms, such as fabrics, pointe shoes or items from the armoury (we use a lot of swords and firearms in both opera and ballet). Surprising objects are sometimes suspended above the Linbury staircase, such as a giant glossy cherry inspired by the one that appears on the roof of the witch's house in our production of Humperdinck's opera *Hansel and Gretel*. The spaces have to be functional and flexible for different events, but I revel in the moments when we can add a grace note, such as the detailed model boxes that we create before building a set or a beautiful costume worn by a dancer.

' they turn sketches into the most remarkable three-dimensional objects '

Our props are built on site, in a room flooded with natural light that feels like the most delightful cabinet of curiosities. The light catches certain details: sequins used for glossy peacock feathers, a brass oil lamp, or the glistening, watchful eye of a crocodile. I am always taken aback by the creativity and wit of the team as I walk through the surreal array of props. Alongside masks, severed heads and puppets are tempting banquets that make you forget they're made of polystyrene, fibreglass, latex and paint. It would not be unusual to see life-size trees and even cars waiting in a vice, half made. The props team are artists, but also engineers and welders. They use complex machinery and powerful chemicals every day in a fusion of science and art as they turn sketches into the most remarkable three-dimensional objects that are created to enhance a performance.

While props are made in Covent Garden, sets are built and backdrops painted at the Bob and Tamar Manoukian Production Workshop in Essex. Situated in High House Production Park, alongside our Costume Centre, the workshop was purpose-built for the Royal Opera House and designed to accommodate the sets and scenery of several productions at once. It includes a paint shop, metal workshop and a production area as large as the main Covent Garden stage, allowing the creative team to construct the entire set before transferring it to London. It is a hugely significant part of what we do, and one that is largely invisible to visitors.

> 'working to create something extraordinary out of thin air'

Although no two days at the Royal Opera House are the same, almost every night of the year the curtain rises on one or both of our stages. Hundreds of dedicated people spend months working to create something extraordinary out of thin air. Although there's a score, there's certainly not a formula, and to bring everything together is phenomenally challenging, all-consuming, even magical. The choreography of the set turnaround in the hours between a stage rehearsal and a performance is just one of the challenges facing our staff, with very little time to spare. That said, there's nothing like the collective jolt of adrenaline that comes from ensuring a live performance is successful, despite the inevitable surprises thrown our way: a sick performer, perhaps, or a malfunctioning set, or even a localized power cut that takes out a swathe of Covent Garden. We once had to endure the last of these halfway through the first act of a performance of *Così fan tutte*, which meant that we were unable to move the scenery. Instead, we managed to stage a coherent performance on a single, unchanging set, thanks to the ingenuity of the cast and crew, who were cheered to the rafters for their efforts.

' I was profoundly inspired by the whole experience '

The audience experience doesn't start when the lights go down; it begins the moment you enter the building, and I pay close attention to what people may or may not be enjoying. As night falls and lights illuminate the magnificent Paul Hamlyn Hall, it feels as if the opera house itself is tuning up, full of glow and anticipation. While we have a lot of audience members who attend frequently, there are also many who join us for the first time as a special treat. There is no requirement to dress up or to spend money on an expensive ticket, so the evening can be as formal or informal as you wish. My first visit was as an eleven-year-old child with my mother because the babysitter had fallen through. It perhaps wasn't immediately obvious that a standing place for *The Valkyrie* (the second opera in Wagner's *Ring* cycle) would be the ideal way to introduce a young person to the art of opera, but I was profoundly inspired by the whole experience. While enveloped in that glorious atmosphere, the music was brought to life on stage by the most extraordinary forces, and that was the start of a lifelong interest.

The main auditorium holds so many memories. In the last couple of years of my brother's life we spent a large amount of time together, developing a love of ballet. When he died, I was able to name one of our favourite standing places in his memory. It's just above the Director's Box, so I always have the sense that he is looking down from the lower slips.

'*gripping drama, emotional truth and divine music*'

The main auditorium is like the inside of a velvet jewellery box. The warm lighting enlivens the gilt details, including the elegant statues that watch over the audience. The space is breathtaking in its splendour: one of my favourite sounds is the collective gasp of schoolchildren as they see the space for the first time at the beginning of a Schools' Matinée, although just as uplifting are their untrammelled cheers at the end of a performance. Stamping and screams aren't what most people expect to hear in an opera house, offering a healthy corrective to those who think that opera and ballet are lacking in relevance. There is gripping drama, emotional truth and divine music in these performances, often so arresting that time itself seems to stand still. This impact is what keeps it relevant, whether the works being performed were written two months or more than two hundred years ago.

all are artists of the first order

Music and performance really are the beating life force of the building. At any point in the day I may turn a corner and hear melodies coming from one of the multitude of small rehearsal rooms where artists are assiduously working together. We have around forty-five pianos in the building – quite a task for the piano tuner. There are four ballet rehearsal rooms where dancers and choreographers perfect moves to great exactitude. There are three music rehearsal rooms, one specifically for our chorus and two for opera singers to work with the sets. Our most important rehearsal spaces are, of course, the stages themselves, where all the elements are brought together, driven by the engine of the orchestra in the pit. The horseshoe shape of the main auditorium allows for seating immediately to the left and right of the stage, from where you can be almost as transfixed by the musicians as by the performers. The scale and elements of the orchestra vary widely according to each performance: a contemporary work by George Benjamin will require something quite different to one by Richard Strauss. I have seen (and heard) everything, from glass harmonicas to a wind machine, from several pianos to anvils. We are lucky enough to attract our musicians and conductors from around the world, and all are artists of the first order.

The sequence of moments before a performance begins – the audience taking their seats, the orchestra warming up, the lights beginning to dim – still have an exhilarating charge for me. The combination of sublime beauty and the constant potential for things to go wrong is an extreme sport. In this space, reputations are made and the works of great artists, both contemporary and historic, are presented anew every night. It is little short of a miracle that the teams manage to accomplish what they do each day. Curtain calls are often emotional: watching performers who have given their all face the audience and receive their thanks is a deeply affecting moment. And then it's over. The audience streams out into the night, and some time afterwards I'll make my way home, happy in the knowledge that there will be another great performance tomorrow.

LINBURY THEATRE

LINBURY TH

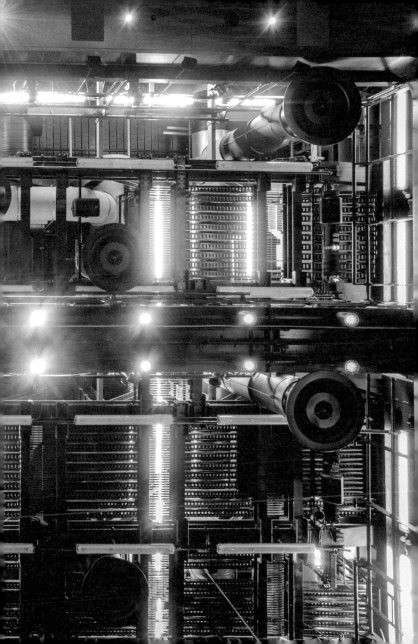

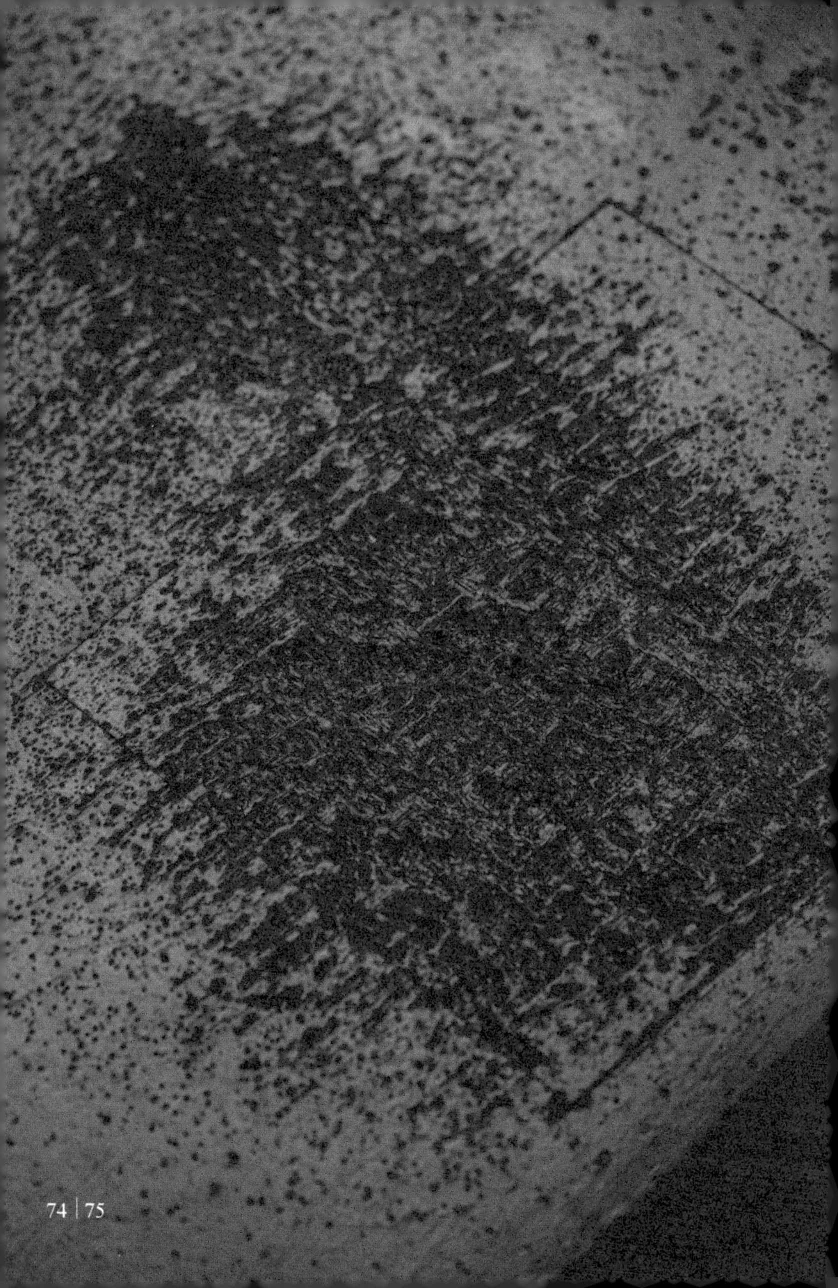

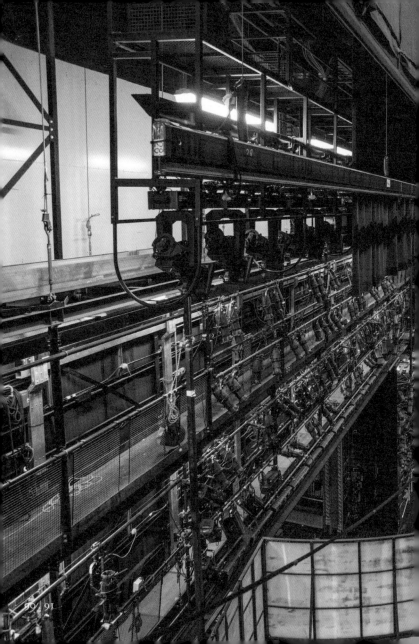

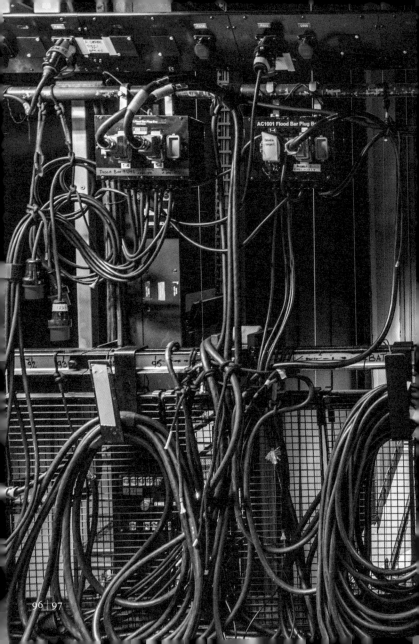

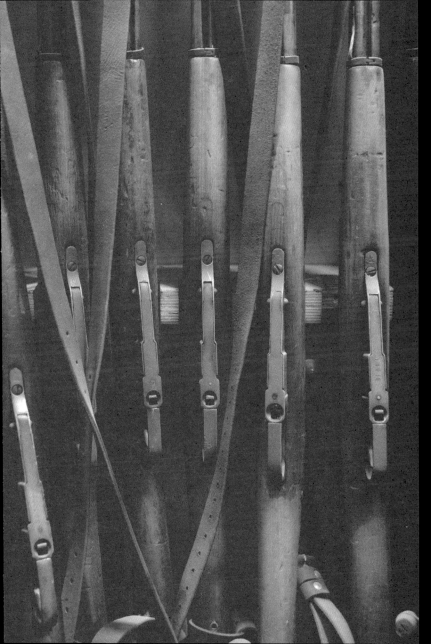

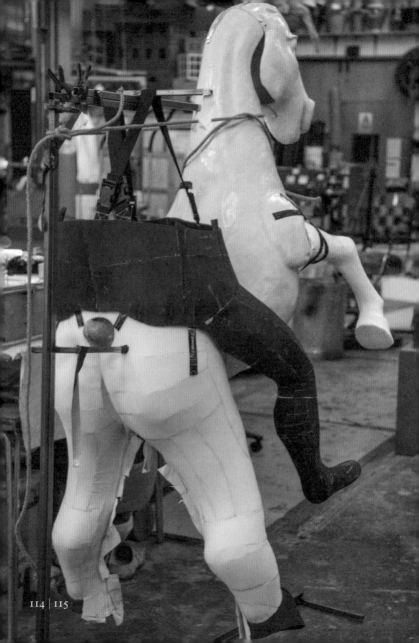

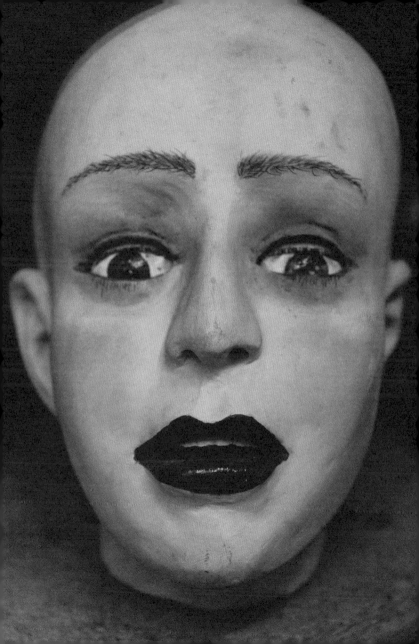

GENERAL USE

2018

⚠️ (!)

ARIN RED DYE

NT BINDER

BLOOD

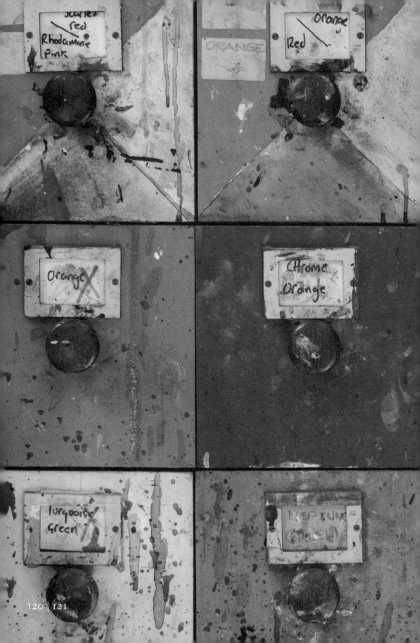

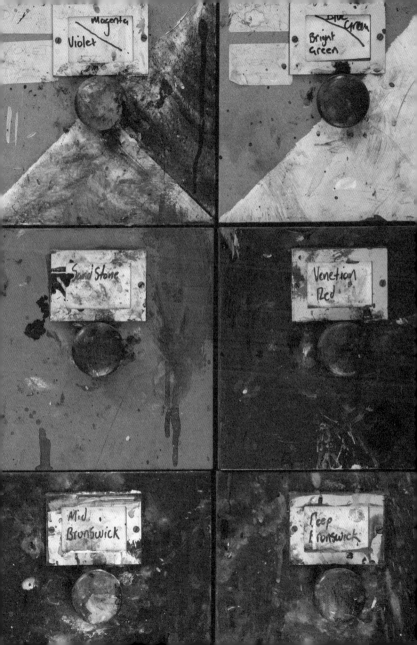

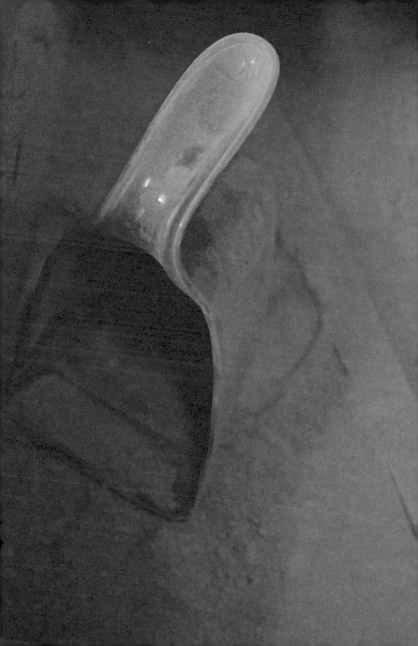

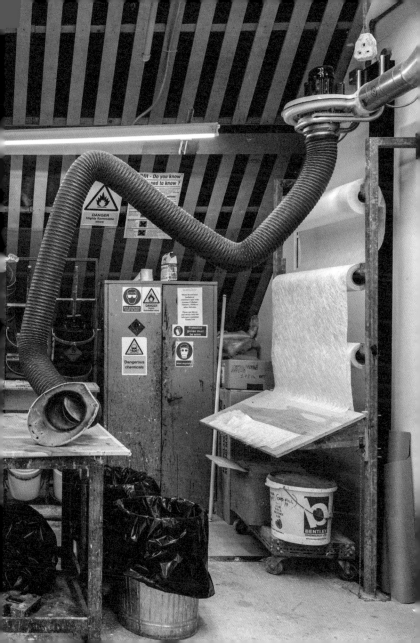

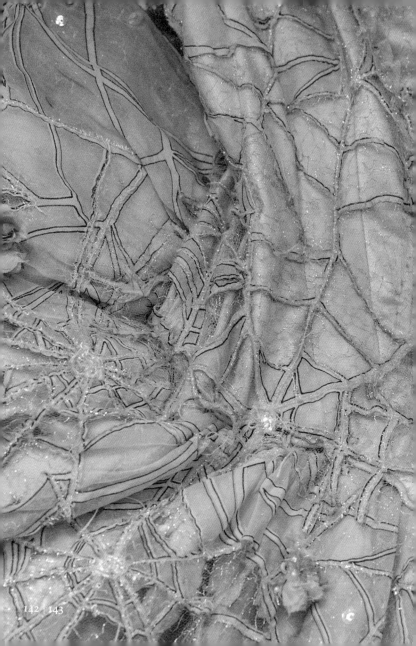

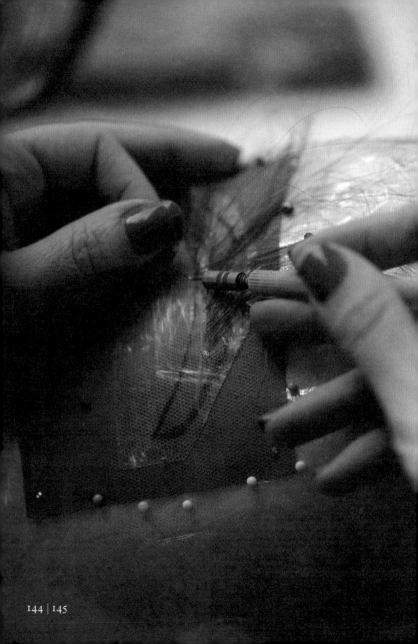

OSIPOVA

CUTH&EXLSON

CAPTIONS

Frontispiece: The main auditorium of the Royal Opera House (the third opera house on the site and completed in 1858) is the largest Victorian theatre in London, seating 2,256 people in a tiered horseshoe arrangement before a proscenium stage.

Page 4: The ground-floor Link Corridor, leading from the main entrance to the Crush Room, incorporates a number of beautiful scale models by Hannah Taylor representing earlier theatres on the Royal Opera House site. This model depicts the opening night of the Royal Italian Opera (as the previous building on the site became known) on 6 April 1847, with a performance of Rossini's opera *Semiramide* with leading Italian soprano Giulia Grisi (1811–1869) in the title role. The Royal Italian Opera was completely destroyed by fire on 5 March 1856. (*See also caption to pages 42–43 below.*)

Pages 14–15: The Royal Opera House sits in the heart of Covent Garden, offering visitors to the upper levels of the foyer extensive views over the glazed roof of the covered market, designed in a neoclassical style by Charles Fowler in 1830.

Pages 16–20: The classical façade of the Royal Opera House, overlooking Bow Street, was designed by Edward Middleton Barry (son of Sir Charles Barry, architect of the Palace of Westminster). Its most prominent feature is a large neoclassical portico featuring six Corinthian columns. The frieze behind the portico, an important work by the great sculptor John Flaxman RA (1755–1826) and dating from *c.* 1809, was rescued from the previous opera house on the site, which burnt down in 1856.

Pages 21–27: The Paul Hamlyn Hall, formerly known as the Floral Hall, was designed by Edward Middleton Barry to serve as a flower, fruit and vegetable market that would provide his rebuilt Royal Opera House of 1858 with a source of income. Renamed in 2007 after benefactor (and book publisher) Paul Hamlyn, the hall has been magnificently restored and now houses the Champagne Bar and Balconies Restaurant.

Pages 28–33: The Linbury Foyer was created in 2018 by architects Stanton Williams as part of their extensive redevelopment of the Royal Opera House. The elegant space, finely crafted from marble, American black walnut and patinated brass, is open all day, bringing to the foyer a sense of energy that continues long into the night.

Pages 34–41: The Linbury Theatre, originally built in the 1990s to designs by Dixon Jones architects working with Building Design Partnership (BDP) and fully refurbished in 2018 by architects Stanton Williams, provides the Royal Opera House with a state-of-the-art 406-seat auditorium of outstanding quality, and is ideal for more intimate or experimental ballet and opera productions.

Pages 42–43: This scale model in the Link Corridor by Hannah Taylor depicts the auditorium of the Theatre Royal, Covent Garden, in 1804 – the first playhouse on the site of the Royal Opera House – showing the well-known actor John Philip Kemble (1757–1823) on stage in the title role of Sheridan's play *Pizarro*. The Theatre Royal was destroyed by fire in 1808. (*See also caption to page 4, above.*)

Pages 44–51: The opulent Crush Room of 1858 has recently been fully restored. Gilded, mirrored and illuminated by crystal chandeliers, this impressive dining-room is lined with paintings, the majority by the Dutch artist Augustinus Terwesten (1649–1711).

Pages 52–53: The spotlit, wood-panelled corridor leading to the boxes of the auditorium introduces a sense of drama even before the performance has begun.

Pages 54–69: The crimson-and-gold interior of the main auditorium has been the setting of world-class opera and ballet productions since 1858. The proscenium arch, 12.3 metres (40 feet 4 inches) high and 14.8 metres (48 feet 6 inches) wide, can be narrowed by 2 metres (6 feet 6 inches) by adjusting the inner pair of gilded barleycorn twists flanking the stage. The house curtains, adorned with the insignia of Her Majesty The Queen, weigh almost 3 tons. The gilt-and-plaster frieze about the proscenium arch depicts mythological scenes, with a central medallion showing a profile portrait of Queen Victoria. The auditorium is overlooked by the Royal Box, situated just to the right of the stage (pages 56–57).

Pages 70–71: A vertiginous view of the main auditorium, viewed through the oculus of the shallow ceiling dome.

Pages 72–75: The Orchestra of the Royal Opera House, founded in 1946, plays in the pit for nearly every performance of The Royal Opera and The Royal Ballet. The marks left over time by cello spikes have given the pit floor a sculptural texture and patina (page 74).

Pages 76–79: The Royal Opera Chorus, founded in 1946, has its own rehearsal space near the main stage.

Pages 80–83: The Royal Opera House employs a large team of highly skilled make-up technicians, who prepare each performer for their role, whether for opera or ballet.

Pages 84–85: Singers from the Royal Opera Chorus make their way to the main stage in full costume, having received their call from the DSM (Deputy Stage Manager).

Pages 86–87: The performing area of the stage in the main auditorium covers 245.8 square metres (2,645 square feet) and is 24 metres (78 feet) deep, making it one of the largest stages in the UK.

Pages 88–89: Signs on the floor of the stage are a traditional way of helping the stage crew undertake rapid set changes, while they also help to orientate performers and others in the bewildering backstage environment.

Pages 90–95: The state-of-the-art fly tower of the Royal Opera House is 37 metres (121 feet) tall, and can accommodate the main sets for all the current opera and ballet productions.

Pages 96–99: The electrics department of the Royal Opera House runs a tight ship, with all its equipment carefully and safely stored while offering a dazzling array of technical solutions to meet every possible requirement.

Pages 100–103: Weapons of all types, from swords and daggers to pistols, rifles and machine guns, are required for a surprising number of productions, and are all safely stored in a high-security walk-in safe.

Pages 104–105: The luggage store is able to provide a suitable case – or even a modern supermarket shopping basket – for any opera or ballet production.

Pages 106–115: The on-site props department occupies a fascinating space of organized chaos and creative ingenuity in which the wishes of designers are skilfully interpreted for every production.

Page 116: Stage blood sits ready mixed on a shelf, stored, appropriately, in old tomato purée jars.

Page 117: Paint brushes of every size bear the patina of constant use – symbolizing, perhaps, just how much thought and work goes into the detail of every production.

Pages 118–119: The messy process of dyeing cauldrons of fabric to meet the specific requirements of a costume designer has inadvertently transformed this cooker into an apocalyptic nightmare.

Pages 120–123: Powder paints of every hue are stored in colour-coded drawers, ready to be used on props and scenery.

Pages 124–125: The creative process of making props and sets for each production requires immense skill, while the need to follow well-established health-and-safety guidelines is clearly demonstrated by the hoses that draw away dust and fumes, and through a plethora of official warning signs.

Pages 126–129: A busy team of milliners makes and adjusts hats for every production and individual performer, overseen by rows of model heads of every shape and size.

Pages 130–135: The Royal Opera House has separate costume departments for men and women, but they both have at their disposal a vast and well-organized array of haberdashery and fabrics.

Pages 136–141: The highly skilled staff in the busy costume departments work closely with the costume designer of each opera or ballet, bringing couture standards and extraordinary levels of craftsmanship to each production. It is a tradition at the Royal Opera House to sew into the back of each costume a small label that records the role for which it was made, as well as the names of those who have performed it in each production and its revival (pages 138–139).

Pages 144–147: When required for a production, wigs are made to fit each individual singer or dancer, using a cast of their head that is then covered with lace before strands of hair are carefully sewn into place. The process is skilled and time-consuming, but the results are utterly transformative and convincing.

Pages 148–149: The Royal Opera House has a small but busy footwear department. Here, a soft and supple leather boot is being prepared for a member of the corps de ballet.

Pages 150–153: High above Floral Street, the 'rotating' Bridge of Aspiration (2003), designed by architects Wilkinson Eyre, provides a graceful connection between The Royal Ballet School and the Royal Opera House that evokes the movement of a dancer.

THE ROYAL OPERA HOUSE: A BRIEF HISTORY

7 December 1732: The first theatre on the site of the present Royal Opera House is opened, with a production of William Congreve's *The Way of the World*. Called the Theatre Royal, and constructed on the site of a former convent garden, the new playhouse was designed by architect Edward Shepherd (who also designed the well-known district of Mayfair known, eponymously, as Shepherd Market).

1734: The Theatre Royal presents its first ballet, *Pygmalion*. In the same year it also presents its first opera, *Il pastor fido*, by George Frederick Handel. Several of Handel's operas, including *Alcina* and *Ariodante* (both 1735) and *Atalanta* (1736), receive their premières at the Theatre Royal.

20 September 1808: The Theatre Royal, Covent Garden, is destroyed by fire.

18 September 1809: The second Theatre Royal on the site, designed by Robert Smirke (architect of the British Museum), opens with a performance of Shakespeare's play *Macbeth*.

1817: Gaslight replaces candles and oil lamps to illuminate productions on stage.

1837: The Theatre Royal becomes the first theatre to use limelight, an intense form of illumination created by directing an oxyhydrogen flame at a cylinder of quicklime (calcium oxide). This allows individual performers to be picked out using spotlights, the electrical versions of which continue to be referred to, in theatre parlance, as 'limes'.

1846: The Theatre Royal auditorium is destroyed by fire, although the main structure of the building remains largely intact.

6 April 1847: The theatre reopens as the Royal Italian Opera House, with a performance of Rossini's *Semiramide*. For the next 45 years all operas at Covent Garden are sung in Italian, even if originally written in French, German or English.

5 March 1856: The Royal Italian Opera House is again completely destroyed by fire.

15 May 1858: The new Royal Italian Opera House opens – the third theatre building on the site – to designs by architect Edward Middleton Barry, third son of Sir Charles Barry, who designed the Palace of Westminster. The opening production is of Giacomo Meyerbeer's *Les Huguenots*. Barry also designed the adjacent Floral Hall (renamed the Paul Hamlyn Hall in 2007), which was originally intended to serve as a flower, fruit and vegetable market that would provide the rebuilt opera house with a secondary source of income.

8 June 1892: The Covent Garden debut of Richard Wagner's *Ring* cycle, conducted by Gustav Mahler, is preceded by a single performance of *Siegfried*. It is the first opera to be sung here in German since 1847, and the theatre is soon after renamed the Royal Opera House.

1914–18: During the First World War the Royal Opera House is requisitioned by the UK government's Office of Works and used as a furniture repository.

1939–45: During the Second World War the lease on the Royal Opera House is taken over by the ballroom chain Mecca, who convert the main auditorium into a dance hall. It becomes one of London's entertainment hotspots.

20 February 1946: The new resident ballet company at the Royal Opera House, Sadler's Wells Ballet (founded 1931), marks the return of the building to its original purpose as a home for ballet and opera with a performance of Marius Petipa's *The Sleeping Beauty*, to music by Pyotr Il'yich Tchaikovsky and in a production designed by Oliver Messel. In the same year, the Orchestra of the Royal Opera House is founded.

14 January 1947: The newly formed Covent Garden Opera Company gives its first performance, of Bizet's *Carmen*.

1956: Sadler's Wells Ballet is granted a Royal Charter, to create The Royal Ballet.

1968: The Covent Garden Opera Company is granted a Royal Charter, to create The Royal Opera.

Mid-1980s: The Royal Opera House undergoes its first major expansion and renovation, to designs by Jeremy Dixon with Building Design Partnership (BDP), resulting in the addition of two new ballet studios, a chorus rehearsal room, an opera rehearsal room, dressing rooms and offices.

1984: Surtitles, involving the projection of the libretto, in English, above the proscenium arch, are introduced for all opera performances.

1997–99: The second phase of the building's transformation, again by architects Dixon Jones with BDP, results in the refurbishment of the main auditorium and foyers, new accommodation for The Royal Opera and The Royal Ballet, a studio theatre (now the Linbury; *see below*), reconstruction of part of the Floral Hall, and the addition of an arcade of shops around the north-east corner of the Covent Garden piazza.

2003: The twisting Bridge of Aspiration, designed by architects Wilkinson Eyre to evoke the graceful movement of a dancer, is opened. Situated high above Floral Street, it connects The Royal Ballet School and the Royal Opera House.

2015–18: A further transformation of the Royal Opera House is undertaken by architects Stanton Williams, opening up the foyer spaces and terraces, providing new bars, cafés and restaurants, and redeveloping the 1990s Linbury Theatre, an intimate space for smaller or more experimental productions by The Royal Ballet and The Royal Opera as well as visiting companies from the UK and abroad.

ACKNOWLEDGMENTS

Thames & Hudson and Harry Cory Wright would like to thank the following for their invaluable help with this book: Jane Storie, Ellen West, John Snelson, Imogen Nolan, Olivia Sangster-Bullers and all the staff of the Royal Opera House, who gave much of their time to the project and were so cooperative during the photo shoots.

First published in the United Kingdom in 2020 by Thames & Hudson Ltd, 181A High Holborn, London WC1V 7QX

Royal Opera House © 2020 Thames & Hudson Ltd, London

Photographs © 2020 Harry Cory Wright
Introduction © 2020 Alex Beard

Series book design by Peter Dawson, gradedesign.com

British Library Cataloguing-in-Publication Data
A catalogue record for this book is available from the British Library

ISBN 978-0-500-29579-3

Printed and bound in China by C&C Offset Printing Co. Ltd